Animals in Danger in Asia

Louise and Richard Spilsbury

Raintree is an imprint of Capstone Global Library Limited, a company incorporated in England and Wales having its registered office at 7 Pilgrim Street, London, EC4V 6LB – Registered company number: 6695582

www.raintreepublishers.co.uk
myorders@raintreepublishers.co.uk

Text © Capstone Global Library Limited 2013
First published in hardback in 2013
Paperback edition first published in 2014
The moral rights of the proprietor have been asserted.

Edited by Rebecca Rissman, Dan Nunn, and Adrian Vigliano
Designed by Philippa Jenkins
Picture research by Tracy Cummins
Originated by Capstone Global Library Ltd
Printed in China by South China Printing Company Ltd

ISBN 978 1 406 26206 3 (hardback)
17 16 15 14 13
10 9 8 7 6 5 4 3 2 1

ISBN 978 1 406 26213 1 (paperback)
18 17 16 15 14
10 9 8 7 6 5 4 3 2 1

British Library Cataloguing in Publication Data
A full catalogue record for this book is available from the British Library.

Acknowledgements
We would like to thank the following for permission to reproduce photographs: AP Photo p. 27 (Courtesy of Zeb Hogan, University of Nevada-Reno); FLPA p. 10 (Imagebroker); Getty Images pp. 18 (Tom McHugh), 19 (Mark Carwardine), 29 (Tim Platt); Nature Picture Library pp. 9 (© Wild Wonders of Europe/ Shpilenok), 15 (© Hanne & Jens Eriksen); Newscom p. 23 (Dinodia); NHPA p. 13 (Martin Zwick); Shutterstock pp. 4 (© Chris P.), 5 bottom (© tororo reaction), 5 top (© Pichugin Dmitry), 6 (© BlueOrange Studio), 11 (© Pichugin Dmitry), 22 (© Uryadnikov Sergey), 25 (©Regien Paassen), icons (© Florian Augustin), (© tristan tan), maps (© AridOcean); Superstock pp. 14 (© Animals Animals), 17 (© Minden Pictures), 21 (© Minden Pictures), 26 (© age footstock), 28 (© Minden Pictures).

Cover photograph of a gavial crocodile reproduced with permission of Shutterstock (© Jody).
Cover photograph of a mountain in Thailand reproduced with permission of Shutterstock (© jnara).
Cover photograph of a giant panda bear reproduced with permission of Shutterstock (© Hung Chung Chih).
Cover photograph of a Sumatran tiger reproduced with permission of Shutterstock (© neelsky).
Cover photograph of a Bali mynah reproduced with permission of Shutterstock (© Laurent Ruelle).

We would like to thank Michael Bright for his invaluable help in the preparation of this book.

Every effort has been made to contact copyright holders of any material reproduced in this book. Any omissions will be rectified in subsequent printings if notice is given to the publisher.

Contents

Some words are shown in bold, **like this.** You can find out what they mean by looking in the glossary.

Where is Asia?

We divide the world into seven large areas of land called **continents**. Asia is the largest continent in the world. It covers almost a third of the world's land area.

NORTH AMERICA

EUROPE

ASIA

ATLANTIC OCEAN

AFRICA

PACIFIC OCEAN

PACIFIC OCEAN

SOUTH AMERICA

INDIAN OCEAN

N

W   E

S

AUSTRALIA

ANTARCTICA

Can you see the continent of Asia?

There are many types of landscapes in Asia. There are high mountains, sandy **deserts**, long rivers, thick **rainforests**, and dusty, open **plains**. There are also many islands and long stretches of coast.

Many animals live in Asia's different **habitats**.

Animals of Asia

Some animals in Asia are **endangered**. This means there are very few of that type of animal left. If they all die, that type of animal will be **extinct**. An animal that is extinct is gone from the planet forever.

The unusual proboscis monkey is one of Asia's endangered animals.

Different types of animals look and behave differently from each other. We sort them into groups to help tell them apart.

Animal classification chart

Amphibian	• lives on land and in water • has damp, smooth skin • has **webbed** feet • lays many eggs	
Bird	• has feathers and wings • hatches out of hard-shelled eggs	
Fish	• lives in water • has **fins** and most have **scales** • young hatch from soft eggs	
Mammal	• drinks milk when a baby • has hair on its body	
Reptile	• has scales on its body • lives on land • young hatch from soft-shelled eggs	

Look out for pictures like these next to each photo. They will tell you what type of animal each photo shows.

Northern Asia

There are mountains, **deserts**, and **grasslands** in northern Asia. People dig **mines** and build roads through the **habitats**. Farm animals eat plants in grasslands. People hunt some animals here, too.

This is the northern part of Asia.

ARCTIC OCEAN

PACIFIC OCEAN

URAL MOUNTAINS

ALTAI MOUNTAINS

Lake Baikal

ARAL SEA

Gobi Desert

Taklimakan Desert

TIBETAN PLATEAU

HIMALAYAS

Mount Everest

N
W   E
S

Saiga antelopes live in **herds** in deserts and grasslands. They take turns watching for danger. They can run fast to escape **predators** such as wolves. Farm animals are eating the plants that saiga usually eat.

The saiga antelope has an unusually large nose that hangs down over its mouth!

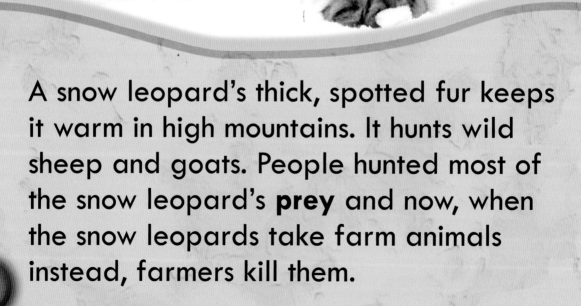

The snow leopard's large paws stop it from sinking in snow.

A snow leopard's thick, spotted fur keeps it warm in high mountains. It hunts wild sheep and goats. People hunted most of the snow leopard's **prey** and now, when the snow leopards take farm animals instead, farmers kill them.

The wild bactrian camel grows thick hair to stay warm in winter, when it is cold in the desert. This hair falls out by summer, so the camel can stay cool. Camels eat plants. Some people hunt the camel for food.

The wild bactrian camel's two toes spread widely to stop it from sinking in desert sand.

Western Asia

Some animals in western Asia are **endangered** because people cut down trees for firewood or to build or farm on the land. Farm animals eat mountain plants, and some mountain **habitats** are destroyed by **mines**.

This map shows the western part of Asia.

BLACK SEA

MEDITERRANEAN SEA

CASPIAN SEA

Euphrates River

Tigris River

AL HIJAZ MOUNTAINS

ELBURZ MOUNTAINS

Lut Desert

PERSIAN GULF

Arabian Desert

ARABIAN SEA

N
W E
S

The Arabian tahr needs mountain plants to eat. It also needs to drink water often. When people take over mountain land, the Arabian tahr cannot travel to new areas to find water when it needs to.

The tahr's rubbery hooves grip rocks so that it can move quickly over mountains.

13

Kaznakow's Caucasian vipers have patterned skin to hide them on forest floors. Then they suddenly attack small mammals that pass by. People cut down vipers' forest homes and catch them for pets.

This viper has hollow fangs that inject **venom** into **prey** to kill it!

This woodpecker pecks holes in bark with its strong beak to feed on insects inside.

The Arabian woodpecker needs trees to survive, too. Its strong beak pecks holes in trees, so the woodpecker can make nests safely inside. Its long, sticky tongue licks ants and other **insects** off tree **bark** to eat.

15

Eastern Asia

In eastern Asia, people are cutting down forests. They are building **dams** that block rivers and reduce the number of fish other animals can eat. Fishing and ferry boats also injure or kill animals.

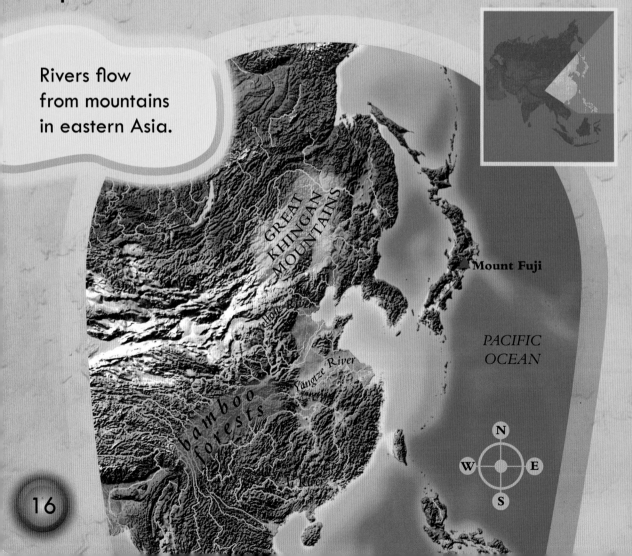

Rivers flow from mountains in eastern Asia.

GREAT KHINGAN MOUNTAINS

Yellow River

Mount Fuji

PACIFIC OCEAN

Yangtze River

bamboo forests

N E S W

The giant panda eats mostly bamboo. It has powerful **jaws** and wide, flat teeth to chew this tough plant. People cut down bamboo forests, and roads and villages stop pandas from getting to other forests.

Giant pandas spend 10 to 16 hours each day eating!

The Chinese giant salamander lives in dark holes in rocks in fast-flowing mountain streams. It uses smell and touch to find fish, snails, and other **prey** at night. Then it snaps them up in its wide mouth.

People hunt this 2-metre- (6-foot-) long salamander for food.

Fishermen kill baiji by using electricity to kill fish in the Yangtze River, where it lives.

The baiji makes beeps, clicks, and whistling sounds. Then it uses the echoes that bounce back to find fish in dark water at night. It snatches them up in its long, narrow beak and swallows them whole!

19

Southern Asia

People are cutting down grass and trees in southern Asia and putting up new houses, roads, and farms on the land. People also build on riverbanks and take river water for homes, factories, and farms.

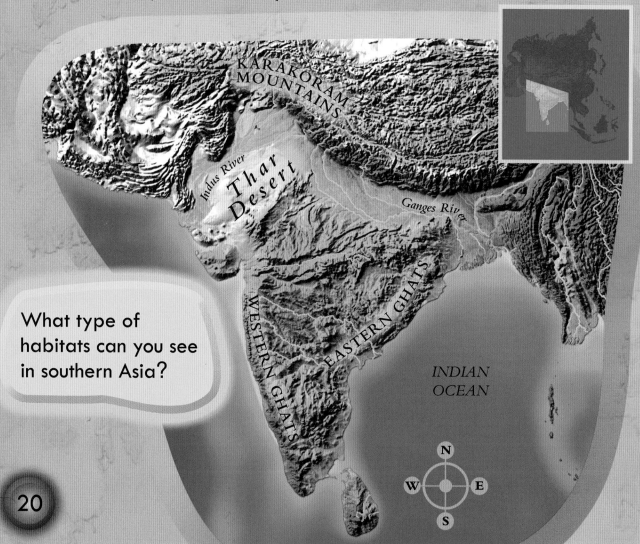

KARAKORAM MOUNTAINS

Indus River

Thar Desert

Ganges River

WESTERN GHATS

EASTERN GHATS

INDIAN OCEAN

N
W E
S

What type of habitats can you see in southern Asia?

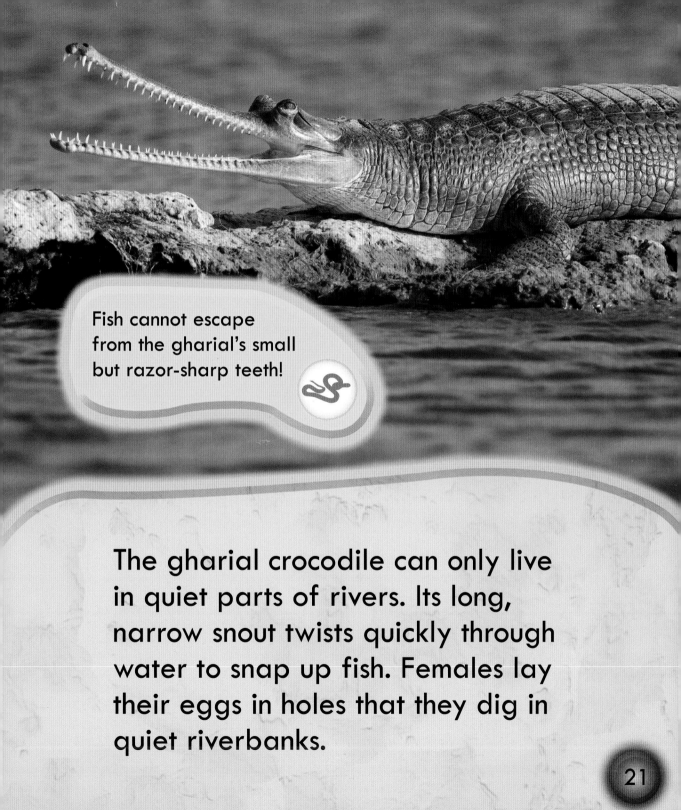

Fish cannot escape from the gharial's small but razor-sharp teeth!

The gharial crocodile can only live in quiet parts of rivers. Its long, narrow snout twists quickly through water to snap up fish. Females lay their eggs in holes that they dig in quiet riverbanks.

A tiger's stripes help it to hide in long grass as it sneaks up on **prey**.

Tigers use their sharp claws and teeth to catch deer that feed on grass. With less grass, there are fewer deer. People also hunt tigers to sell their skins and to make medicine from their bones.

Great Indian bustards are tall, heavy birds that need **grasslands** to survive. They eat plant seeds and berries, and **insects** that feed on plants. Females lay a single egg in a nest on open ground.

Females sit on their egg and care for the chick that hatches out of it.

Southeast Asia

Plants grow well in Southeast Asia because it is hot and wet most of the year. People have cut down many of the thick forests here to sell the wood, to grow crops such as rice and fruit, and to build houses.

tropical forest

Mekong River

SOUTH CHINA SEA

Mount Kinabalu

tropical forest

Equator

INDIAN OCEAN

Southeast Asia is made up of a strip of mainland and many islands.

Elephants use their trunk to spray water over themselves to keep cool!

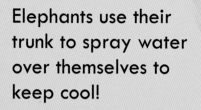

Elephants need forests to survive. They use their tusks to peel bark from trees and to dig for roots to eat. They use their trunk to pull up plants to eat and to put them in their mouth.

The Bornean orangutan lives in trees. It clambers between branches, finding fruit and leaves to eat. At night, it bends leafy branches over to make a nest on which to sleep, high in the trees.

Young orangutans learn to climb and where to find fruit from their mothers.

The sharp end of the stingray's tail breaks predators' skin and puts venom in it!

The Mekong freshwater stingray can grow to 4 metres (13 feet) long! It skims along the riverbed eating crabs and clams. Many of these stingrays die when they get trapped in fishing nets.

Helping Asia's animals

Some countries in Asia protect animals in **reserves**. These are places where animals can live safely. There are only around 400 Asiatic lions left in the wild, and they all live in the Gir forest reserve.

Without reserves, animals like these Asiatic lions would die out.

You can help **endangered** animals, too! One reason people cut down trees is to make paper. Help by using less paper, by **recycling** paper, and by buying recycled paper.

If we all use less paper, people will cut down fewer trees.

Glossary

bark outer covering of a tree

continent one of seven large areas that make up the world's land

dam barrier that holds back water on a river

desert hot, dry area of land often covered with sand and few plants

endangered when a type of animal is in danger of dying out

extinct no longer alive; not seen in the wild for 50 years

fin flap of skin that helps a fish swim

grassland area of land mainly covered in grass

habitat place where plants and animals live

herd group of animals

insect small animal with six legs, such as an ant or fly

jaws part of an animal's body that contains its mouth and teeth

mine deep hole in the ground dug by people to get coal or metals

plain large area of flat land with few trees

predator animal that catches and eats other animals for food

prey animal that gets caught and is eaten by other animals

rainforest forest of very tall trees in hot, sunny, wet places

recycle to change waste into something we can use

reserve large area of land where plants and animals are protected

scale small, overlapping pieces that cover an animal's body

venom poisonous liquid

webbed when feet have skin between the toes

Find out more

Books

Asia's Most Amazing Animals (Animal Top Tens), Anita Ganeri (Raintree, 2008)

Endangered Animals (Trailblazers), David Orme (Ransom Publishing, 2009)

Internet sites

gowild.wwf.org.uk

Go Wild is the children's club of WWF. You can learn about different animals and their habitats.

www.oum.ox.ac.uk/thezone/animals/extinct/index.htm

Find out about some animals that are now extinct on this website.

Index